ABC Triplets at the Zoo

ABC Triplets at the Zoo

By Ida DeLage

Drawings by Lori Pierson

GARRARD PUBLISHING COMPANY
CHAMPAIGN, ILLINOIS

Library of Congress Cataloging in Publication Data

DeLage, Ida.
    ABC triplets at the zoo.

    (Her Once upon an ABC)
    SUMMARY: The ABC triplets take an alphabetical
walk through the zoo with the 26 letters highlighted
by animals' names and zoo adventures.
    [1. Alphabet. 2. Zoological gardens—Fiction]
I. Pierson, Lori. II. Title. III. Series.

PZ7.D3698Aal   [E]   79-13265
ISBN 0-8116-4357-3

ABC Triplets at the Zoo

We are
the ABC triplets.
We are going
to the ABC Zoo.

There it is!
There is the ABC Zoo.

A ANIMALS

We can see
many **ANIMALS**
at the ABC Zoo.

B BEAR

Come out, **BEAR**.

Come out and see us.

C CAMEL

The **CAMEL**
has big feet.

D DUCKS

The **DUCKS**
swim in the pond
at the ABC Zoo.

E **ELEPHANT**

The **ELEPHANT**
likes peanuts.

F FEED

We can **FEED** the deer
at the ABC Zoo.

G GIRAFFE

The **GIRAFFE**

has a long, long neck.

H HIPPO

Hello, **HIPPO**.

You are fat, fat, fat!

I IGUANA

The **IGUANA**

is sleepy.

J JAGUAR

The **JAGUAR**

has spots.

K KANGAROO

The **KANGAROO** hops.

L LUNCH

We like to have
LUNCH
at the ABC Zoo.

M MONKEY

Hey!

A MONKEY

made a face at us!

N NIGHT OWL

The **NIGHT OWL**
sleeps all day.

O OBEY

OBEY the signs
at the ABC Zoo.

P PEACOCK

The **PEACOCK**

shows his tail.

Q QUAIL

Where is the tail
on the **QUAIL**?

R RIDE

A pony **RIDE**
is fun
at the ABC Zoo.

S **SEALS**

The **SEALS**
bark for a fish.

T **TIGER**

The **TIGER** looks like
a big, big cat.

UMBRELLA BIRD

VULTURE

U **UMBRELLA BIRD**

V **VULTURE**

The **UMBRELLA BIRD**
has an **UMBRELLA**
on his head.
The **VULTURE** has nothing
on his head.

W WOLF

The **WOLF** looks like
a big dog.

WATCH OUT FOR THE ZOO TRAIN

ZOO TRAIN

X IS FOR TRAIN CROSSING.

Ding, dong.

Ding, dong.

The ABC zoo train

is coming!

Y YAK

The **YAK**
has long, long hair.

Z ZEBRA

The **ZEBRA** has stripes.

Good-bye.

Good-bye, ABC Zoo.

It was fun to go

to the ABC Zoo.